WOMEN OF FAITH™
STUDY GUIDE SERIES

AMAZING
FREEDOM

FOREWORD BY
MARY GRAHAM

Published by
THOMAS NELSON™
Since 1798

www.thomasnelson.com

Published in Nashville, Tennessee by Thomas Nelson, Inc., P.O. Box 141000, Nashville, Tennessee 37214.

Thomas Nelson, Inc. titles may be purchased in bulk for educational, business, fundraising, or sales promotional use. For information, please email SpecialMarkets@ThomasNelson.com.

ISBN-10: 1-4185-2830-7
ISBN-13: 978-1-4185-2830-0

Printed in China.

07 08 09 10 MT 9 8 7 6 5 4 3 2 1

✦CONTENTS✦

CONTENTS

✦ FOREWORD ✦

For years I traveled to the former Soviet Union, meeting university students and talking with them about faith. Because the Communists tightly controlled the society, our visits were careful, clandestine, and often a little scary. But the students were so delightful and responsive that it was always worth the risk.

Since we didn't know Russian, we sought out students in the English language department of the university. In our initial meetings, the students were more interested in our prowess with the English language than in our personal faith. Most students hadn't had the opportunity to speak with a native English speaker and, once they spotted us on their campus (I admit, we did stand out like sore thumbs!), they scrambled to meet us. Primarily, they wanted us to teach them slang, which was not found in their textbooks. We just visited with them—which they considered an important part of their study, I suppose. I considered it an important part of their eternal destiny!

Perhaps the most fascinating word we ever discussed (and we did so often) was freedom. While most of us see it as one of the most meaningful words in our language, they considered it negative and repugnant based on their Communist upbringing. Simply mentioning the word meant that we were sure to have lively discussions ensue.

Quite honestly, I had trouble finding words to describe to them how wonderful freedom really is. Although it's now been twenty-five years since I had those conversations, I remember them as if they were yesterday. I hear myself saying to Natasha, Svetlana, Olga, Valeria, and Alana, "Freedom is amazing!"

In America and other free countries of the world, national constitutions provide freedom for individuals and groups in society. However, when we know Christ, our freedoms go far beyond that perspective. And the boundaries and restrictions of any government cannot take them away. They are God-given and for all to receive. God gives us freedom to be all He created us to be; freedom to walk through life in a growing, personal relationship with Him; freedom from fear, shame, and all guilt; freedom to love and be loved; freedom to forgive and be forgiven; freedom to give and to receive all that God has for us.

More often than not, we don't quite grasp the freedom we have in Christ. That's why a biblical study of freedom is important. What kind of freedom does God grant us? What does the Bible teach about how we can experience that freedom? How do we grasp the essence of this truth? Our prayer is that you will study and find freedom in Christ the most *amazing* freedom of all, in ANY language.

—Mary Graham

✦ INTRODUCTION ✦

You may have seen her in your own family home movies: a bright, joyful, little girl, dancing in front of the camera in her oversized dress-ups, a bundle of smiles and giggles . . .

Or, stepping up to home plate in the neighborhood girl's softball game, eager to hit the ball over the centerfielder's head, and maybe a little concerned about keeping her uniform clean . . .

Or, standing in awe at the lighted mall Christmas tree, hoping for brightly colored boxes with big gold bows this year . . .

Maybe she was the compassionate little nurse, holding the wounded puppy, stroking its back, allowing a tear to fall without shame . . .

The fearless child standing up for a friend with disabilities against the taunts of schoolyard bullies . . .

The reader buried in a book half as big as she, exploring new concepts and believing that nothing is beyond her grasp . . .

The faith-filled girl curled up in bed, voicing simple words she's sure God hears . . .

She was free.

She was hopeful.

She was a bundle of potential, eager for her future.

You may have lost sight of her, but she still lives inside you. All of the amazing freedoms that the carefree, trusting little girl version of you once believed are still yours to claim. Your loving heavenly Father is calling you to believe . . . once again . . . that He will set you free.

CHAPTER 1

FREEDOM TO DREAM

"ASK, AND IT WILL BE GIVEN TO YOU; SEEK,
AND YOU WILL FIND; KNOCK, AND IT WILL
BE OPENED TO YOU."

Matthew 7:7

Are you daring to dream for something wonderful—something more—something you haven't yet tasted, or tasted fully? Something you've never done? Something you've desired, but have never pursued? Have you ever wished you could cast off all your inhibitions and fears and rush headlong into the future you'd most like to live?

Have you dared to dream of flying—no, soaring!?

Patsy Clairmont knows about such dreams:

> There they were—two huge orange butterflies outside my office window doing acrobatic feats in tandem. I decided to believe they had been sent to dance just for me. Although as I watched them weaving in and out of my flowering shrubs, I wasn't sure if they were flirting, fighting for territory, or just having a wing-ding of a good time—kind of a fluttery game of tag.
>
> Whatever they were doing, it sure looked whimsical. I wished I could shed my work, don wings, and join them as they twirled about the neighborhood

alighting from time to time on daffodils and berry bushes. These majestic monarchs captured my desire to wing my way down the boulevards of life with beauty and grace.

Yesterday, my husband Les and I stopped for a red light and watched a small flock of blackbirds swoop across our vision and land in a nearby tree. Les asked, "Don't you wish sometimes that you could fly?"

Who hasn't wished it or dreamed of it?

— Patsy Clairmont

1. If you could do anything, knowing with certainty that you could not fail (and would not die!) in the attempt, what would it be?

Sometimes we are afraid to reach out and live the life that we believe we have been called to. But fear is no friend. It may seem to protect, but it slowly suffocates.

Sheila Walsh

Do you know what holds you back from making the attempt? What steps might you take to overcome those things that are standing in your way?

$\mathcal{A}$s we "grow up," many of us seem to lose our ability to dream with utter abandon. We begin to question whether our dreams are valid. We begin to feel hesitant about doing things that seem like "flying."

You may be thinking, *I'm not sure my dream is God's will.* But are you sure that it isn't? Does God's Word support it? Has God called or equipped you for it? Do you sense Him opening the door? What's holding you back?

2. What did Jesus tell His disciples in John 16:23–24 about the things we ask of God the Father in Jesus's name?

3. What does Ephesians 3:20 tell us about the degree to which God is able and desires to help us succeed in realizing our dreams?

*T*he Bible teaches that many things we do not have in this life, we do not have because we simply don't ask God for them. James 4:2 says clearly, "You do not have because you do not ask." God desires that we *ask* Him for help in all things—asking Him to give us His desires and dreams, and then give us the courage to pursue them.

4. The Bible presents a clear balance between what we are to ask and how we are to ask it. What do the verses below reveal about the dreams God desires to fulfill in our lives?

Matthew 21:22

John 15:7–8

James 4:3

"But," you may be saying, "I gave up all my rights to dream when I made mistakes in my past. Those mistakes will surely keep me from having the life I've always dreamed of." Many women seem afraid to pursue their deepest dreams because of something in their past. They are hounded by shame or guilt, even though they know in their hearts that God has forgiven them. The good news is that God's forgiveness is complete!

The Bible tells the story of a woman who dared to dream of a better life for her future, even though her past seemed to give her no right to dream. Jesus encountered her at a well outside her town, Sychar. She was a Samaritan woman, a woman considered to be a half-breed, of poor spiritual pedigree in the eyes of most Jews.

Jesus asked her to draw a drink of water for Him from the well, and then He said to her, "If you knew the gift of God, and who it is who says to you, 'Give Me a drink,' you would have asked Him, and He would have given you living water" (John 4:10). Jesus offered her water that would satisfy her thirst for the rest of her life, and it would give her everlasting life! He was not speaking of literal water, but about meeting her deepest emotional and spiritual needs. He was addressing her inner "thirst" for love, security, and value.

As they conversed, this woman admitted to Jesus that she had had five husbands, and that she was not married

> *I don't know about you, but I want to do more than survive life. It's not enough to just flap my wings a little before I hit the ground and get plowed under. I want to mount up like the eagle and glide over rocky crags, nest in the tallest trees, dive for nourishment in the deepest of mountain lakes, and soar on the wings of the wind.*
>
> Barbara Johnson

to the man with whom she was currently living. She was a woman with a "past."

5. In what ways can you relate to this woman from Sychar? Is there a mistake in your past that you keep repeating? Is it a mistake that has kept you from pursuing a dream?

My friend, remember to take this life one day at a time. When several days attack you, don't give up. A successful woman takes the bricks the devil throws at her and uses them to lay a firm foundation. We all need enough trials to challenge us, enough challenges to strengthen us, and enough strength to do our part in making this a better place to live and love.

Barbara Johnson

6. In what ways might unfulfilled dreams be the cause of your tension, anxiety, or frustration?

7. What do the verses below tell you about God's ability to forgive and heal your past?

Isaiah 1:18–19

Psalm 86:5

John 10:10

*T*he woman at the well was the first person in the Gospels to whom Jesus openly revealed that He was the Messiah (see John 4:25–26). Jesus revealed His identity as He let her know that He knew her identity—completely. She later told the people of her town, "He told me all that I ever did" (see John 4:29). As a result of her telling the people of Sychar about Jesus, He was invited into their midst for two days, and many in that place came to believe Him to be the Christ, the Savior of the world (see John 4:42).

Jesus knew who this woman was in the past, in the present, and who she might be in the future. He knew her dreams, and knew that the...ir fulfillment was ultimately in her relationship with Him as Savior and Lord.

8. How are your dreams and the dreams that God has for you related?

ut, you may be thinking, *I simply don't know* what *to dream. I don't seem to have any real goals, any unfulfilled desires.* Ask God to give you a dream! There are things *He* is dreaming for you. Start dreaming His dreams for your life.

9. What do the verses below challenge you to do?

1 Corinthians 2:9–10

Proverbs 3:5–6

Jeremiah 42:2–3

✦DIGGING DEEPER✦

How important is it to write down what you dream of doing or being? What does Habakkuk 2:2 offer as encouragement? Write down a dream that you feel God may be calling you to pursue. If you don't feel that God has given you a specific dream yet, spend some time in prayer, asking Him to reveal it to you.

✦PONDER AND PRAY✦

Is it possible that you are not living your "dream" life because you have been too afraid or overwhelmed to ask God to help you discover His dream for your life? How might the Lord be inviting you to pray about this today?

✦ NOTES & PRAYER REQUESTS ✦

CHAPTER 2

FREEDOM FROM PARALYZING FEARS

"WHEN YOU LIE DOWN, YOU WILL NOT BE AFRAID;
YES, YOU WILL LIE DOWN AND YOUR SLEEP
WILL BE SWEET."

Proverbs 3:24

We've all heard the phrase "crippling emotions." The truth is, emotions can shackle a person from moving forward in her life, especially fearful emotions.

How much fear have you allowed to build up in you over the years—perhaps a fear of failure or a fear of rejection? To what degree is fear holding you back from taking the risks to learn . . . to try . . . to do . . . to speak up . . . to step out . . . to move forward?

A woman who truly walks in freedom toward the fulfillment of her dreams and goals is a woman who has discovered a way of overcoming fears with faith.

Sheila Walsh has written this about fear: "Fear is a ravenous beast that can eat away at our faith and paralyze us until we are unable to move."

1. Have you ever been paralyzed by fear? Recall the experience in a few words or phrases below:

> *Courage and fear—those two attributes are strange bedmates. It would seem impossible to experience both of them at the same time, yet I believe that's the challenge of the Christian life. Fear tells us that life is unpredictable, anything can happen, but faith replies quietly, "Yes, but God is in Control."*
>
> Sheila Walsh

How did you find yourself able to "move" again?

$\mathcal{F}$aith is the true opposite of fear. The Bible states repeatedly that trusting in the Lord—believing that the Lord will impart His presence and help—is the sure-fire way to overcome fear and experience courage.

2. Note next to each verse or passage below, your insights into what the Bible says about fear:

2 Timothy 1:7

Psalm 31:13–14

Hebrews 13:5b–6

3. When you think about the goals you'd like to achieve, what fears do you have about the pursuit of those goals?

Now take a look at each fear on your list and ask: "What would God like me to do about this fear?" Write down your response next to the fear you have listed.

4. Think about a time when you failed in the past. What were the immediate emotions and consequences of that failure? Did you allow a long-term fear to develop?

The best advice in order to face each day is this: Hope for the best, get ready for the worst, and then take whatever God sends.

Barbara Johnson

Why do you think we fear failure so much?

The Bible tells the story of a woman who decided she had had enough of her illness and went to Jesus for healing. She no doubt had fears about what she was planning to do. She had experienced "a flow of blood" for twelve years, very likely a form of endometriosis or some other disorder in her uterus that caused nonstop menstruation or hemorrhage. She was very likely physically weak. She was also desperate. She had spent all the resources she had trying to find a cure. The Bible says she had been to many physicians and had "suffered" at their hands and was no better, but rather, she grew worse. Then she heard about Jesus. Somewhere inside her a flicker of faith was fanned into flame and she said to herself: "If only I may touch His clothes, I shall be made well." She boldly maneuvered her way through a crowd of people and reached out to touch the hem of Jesus's garment. The Bible says that the flow of blood "dried up" immediately (see Mark 5:25–34).

5. How do you think you would have responded to your situation if you had been in this woman's position?

Have you ever been so desperate in your circumstances that you knew you had to take action, no matter the consequences to your reputation, your pride, or your social standing? What happened as a result of your desperation?

This woman who was hemorrhaging had more than a physical ailment. She also suffered from rejection and, very likely, loneliness. Her condition made her "unclean" in her community at that time, which meant she was required to refrain from mingling with crowds of people or participating in religious ceremonies. For twelve years, she had been isolated from many of her neighbors and friends, and she was prohibited from taking part in many family celebrations. After she touched the hem of Jesus's garment, Jesus turned and asked, "Who touched My clothes?" The woman, "fearing and trembling," fell down at Jesus's feet and told Him the whole truth. He said to her, "Daughter, your faith has made you well. Go in peace, and be healed of your affliction" (see Mark 5:30–34).

6. What advantages do you see in telling Jesus the "whole truth" about your situation, including your fears?

Why would a person be reluctant to admit the whole truth to anybody about her fears . . . perhaps even refusing to admit the whole truth to herself?

What freedom is gained when you confront your fears?

Fear is indiscriminate. It affects all of us regardless of our age or position in life. Whether our fear is absolutely realistic or out of proportion in our minds, our greatest refuge is Jesus Christ.

Luci Swindoll

onfronting our fears and putting our trust in God can release God's peace into our hearts. Barbara Johnson writes:

> Looking through the windows, [Veronica's family] could see the ferocity of the storm. Meteorologists say the most destructive winds of a hurricane occur along the east wall, and that's the part of the eye that walloped their area. Then, as if the hurricane itself wasn't enough, the storm spun off several tornadoes that swirled around them as well. Outside, the world was turned upside down, and the noise was deafening. Yet inside their wood-frame home, which Veronica and Karl had renovated with eleven-inch-thick walls, there was quiet peace. . . . In fact, they felt such peace they all eventually went to bed and slept soundly as the storm blew through. . . .
>
> Now, Veronica doesn't recommend defying official orders and staying put when the authorities tell you to leave. But when you find yourself trapped in a storm with no way out — whatever kind of storm it is — she can tell you how to feel freedom from the fear that, by all accounts, should be part of the experience! "We prayed, and we asked for God's protection," Veronica said, "We knew that whatever came, we could handle it because of our faith in him."
>
> — Barbara Johnson

7. The psalmist writes: "He calms the storm, So that its waves are still" (Psalm 107:29). Have you ever experienced God's peace in a difficult or scary situation—a "storm" of life that may have involved a literal storm, a relationship crisis, a financial crisis, or a health crisis? Recall that situation in a few sentences:

How did God's peace feel to you? Describe it in a few words below.

8. The prophet Isaiah praised God for keeping "in perfect peace all who trust in you, whose thoughts are fixed on you!" (Isaiah 26:3 NLT). In your own words, respond to the following statements.

These are the practical ways I put my "trust" in God (focus on what you do or say):

This is what it means to me to "fix my thoughts" on God:

✦DIGGING DEEPER✦

In what ways does the pursuit of your dreams and purpose involve overcoming fear with faith? How might you "grow in faith" and in your ability to trust God in all things and for all things?

✦PONDER AND PRAY✦

In what ways do you feel challenged to ask God to help you trust Him more about a specific situation you are facing today?

✦ NOTES & PRAYER REQUESTS ✦

✦ NOTES & PRAYER REQUESTS ✦

✦ NOTES & PRAYER REQUESTS ✦

✦ Notes & Prayer Requests ✦

CHAPTER 3

FREEDOM FROM SORROW AND PAINFUL MEMORIES

"The Spirit of the Lord GOD is upon Me,
Because the LORD has anointed Me
To preach good tidings to the poor;
He has sent Me to heal the brokenhearted,
To proclaim liberty to the captives,
And the opening of the prison to those
who are bound."

Isaiah 61:1

Very often we don't know what makes us sad. We just feel a little down. If pushed for an explanation, we might recount a mistake or a situation in which we'd like to call out to the heavens, "Do over!" We might dig deeper and uncover a festering sorrow from the past, perhaps a time of abuse or death or loss.

Grieving takes many forms and can be experienced as the result of many different types of loss—loss of innocence, loss of security, loss of a loved one, loss of opportunity, loss of ability, loss of time or possessions. Every woman's sorrow has a different way of expressing itself and a unique reason for existing.

The woman who walks in freedom is a woman who has learned to trust God to heal her sorrow. And along life's journey, she trusts God to help her carry her burden of compassion for others.

Are you sorrowful today? Are you troubled by old "haunting" memories of past pain or abuse? Do you feel alone in your sorrow?

Often, God will send a friend—usually someone with a similar life experience and pain—to help us in our sorrow. Luci Swindoll writes about this kind of a relationship:

> Jocelyn was a single mother with a six-year-old child. A few weeks after her son had been killed in an automobile accident, Jocelyn met my friend Debbie and they became friends. Every day, Jocelyn simply went to work, came home, ate dinner, and went to bed. Her grief held her captive, and she was unable to overcome the emptiness in her life.
>
> Debbie invited Jocelyn to go on walks with her. They walked, talked, cried together, and got to know each other. One day Debbie planned to have lunch with Joyce, a friend who had also lost a child, and she invited Jocelyn to join them. As they visited, Joyce said, "Jocelyn, you need power to get through this period of your life . . . this loss. You need to know for sure that God is in your life, and you can know that for sure. You simply won't make it without God's power. I know that from my own experience."
>
> Debbie said they all prayed right there at the table, and Jocelyn invited Christ into her heart. "When we left the restaurant, Jocelyn was different," Debbie said. "There was life. It was like somebody had pumped air into a flat tire."
>
> —Luci Swindoll

1. Have you trusted God with *all* your life? In what areas do you perhaps need to invite the Lord to . . .

Heal you?

Comfort you?

> *Each one of us needs a new beginning at some point or another. But it needn't come with a bang of fireworks or a streaking comet. New beginnings often come slowly. They may even sneak up on you—like a tiny ray of sun slipping out from beneath a black cloud. You can be inspired by the smallest thing, so keep your eyes open.*
>
> Barbara Johnson

Strengthen you?

Renew you?

s we noted earlier in this lesson, the prophet Isaiah foretold of Jesus, "The Spirit of the Lord GOD is upon Me, because the LORD has anointed Me to preach good tidings to the poor; He has sent Me to heal the brokenhearted, to proclaim liberty to the captives, and the opening of the prison to those who are bound." (Isaiah 61:1) Jesus may very well have been referring to this verse from the Old Testament when He gave these beatitudes:

"Blessed are the poor in spirit,
> For theirs is the kingdom of heaven.

Blessed are those who mourn,
> For they shall be comforted.

Blessed are the meek [those under yoke and easily directed to go in whatever direction the Lord leads them],
> For they shall inherit the earth." (Matthew 5:3–5)

2. What does it mean to you to be . . .

Poor in spirit?

Brokenhearted?

To be "captive" to a memory or in the prison of an old haunting nightmare?

3. What does it mean to you to . . .

Receive the kingdom of heaven?

Be comforted?

Inherit the earth?

4. In what ways is it possible to preach good tidings to yourself . . . to heal your own broken heart . . . to proclaim liberty to yourself?

Each of us has something broken in our lives: a broken promise, a broken dream, a broken marriage, a broken heart... and we must decide how we're going to deal with our brokenness. We can wallow in self-pity or regret, accomplishing nothing and having no fun or joy in our circumstances; or we can determine with our will to take a few risks, get out of our comfort zone, and see what God will do to bring unexpected delight in our time of need.

Luci Swindoll

In what ways do you need others to help you overcome sorrow or hurtful memories?

The New Testament quotes Jesus speaking to the people from Isaiah, "Today this Scripture is fulfilled in your hearing" (Luke 4:21). Isaiah 61:1 is presented this way in the Gospel of Luke:

> The Spirit of the LORD is upon Me,
> Because He has anointed Me
> To preach the gospel to the poor;
> He has sent Me to heal the brokenhearted,
> To proclaim liberty to the captives
> And recovery of sight to the blind,
> To set at liberty those who are oppressed;
> To proclaim the acceptable year of the LORD.
>
> (Luke 4:18–19)

5. Consider especially these two specific phrases in the passage above:

• "Proclaim . . . recovery of sight to the blind." In what ways do sorrow and hurtful memories keep you from seeing God's goodness or the good future that God has ahead for you?

• "Set at liberty those who are oppressed." In what ways is sorrow, or a haunting hurtful memory, an "oppression"?

*H*annah was a woman who knew what it meant to have two kinds of sorrow. She had the sorrow of being childless, when the most important thing in the world to her was having a baby. She also had the sorrow of continual ridicule—from a rival who had children and knew how to push all of her buttons. Hannah found herself belittled openly and frequently about her inability to conceive a child. She was miserable.

At an annual family feast, Hannah "lost it." She went to the door of the tabernacle—the most holy place she knew to go—and there, in "bitterness of soul," she wept "in anguish." She admitted to the priest who found her there, "I am a woman of sorrowful spirit. I have . . . poured out my soul before the LORD." The priest replied to her, "Go in peace, and the God of Israel grant your petition which you have asked of Him." Hannah returned to the family feast and the Bible tells us "her face was no longer sad" (see 1 Samuel 1:1–18).

6. What does it mean to you to "pour out your soul before the Lord"?

7. What is the specific sorrow that you are asking the Lord to heal in your life?

arbara Johnson certainly has known sorrows in her life. She and her husband had a unique approach to dealing with their sadness. She writes:

You may have heard of my Joy Room, the addition we built onto our mobile home to hold all the funny toys, jokes, plaques, gag gifts, and other smile makers I've collected since two of our sons were killed. The collection grew out of a shoebox I used to hold funny greeting cards, one-liners, and jokes friends sent to me or that I found wherever I traveled. When sadness threatened to overwhelm me, I would open my Joy Box and inevitably find something that made me smile or even laugh out loud.

—Barbara Johnson

8. What might you do—in a very practical and tangible way—to create an atmosphere or environment of joy in your home? In your workplace?

9. What encouragement do you draw from Revelation 21:4?

The disturbing reality is, at times, we all appear to be running... running literally for our lives. We're running from hurtful memories, we're running from relationships that require time and discipline to repair, we're running from various fears we think may overtake us, and we're even running from knowledge of ourselves. I don't have to run to survive. As a matter of fact, I am invited to rest to survive.

Marilyn Meberg

To what extent do you believe these words are for believers in Christ Jesus today?

✦DIGGING DEEPER✦

Sorrows come to every person's life. While we can never pain-proof our lives or prevent all situations that might be hurtful, we can develop a strategy to follow when sorrow and hurt envelop us. Give some thought to the strategy you will choose to pursue when sorrow or painful memories seem to keep you from moving forward in freedom toward the fulfillment of your dreams and purpose on this earth.

✦PONDER AND PRAY✦

Ask the Lord to help you identify the pain that you may have "hidden" in your heart. Then, ask the Lord to heal your broken heart and help you to move beyond your sorrows.

Joy is permanent. Once you have it, you never lose it. It may be overshadowed by human frailties, but real joy lasts for eternity.

Thelma Wells

✦ Notes & Prayer Requests ✦

✦ NOTES & PRAYER REQUESTS ✦

CHAPTER 4

FREEDOM FROM PERFECTIONISM

"WE KNOW THAT ALL THINGS WORK TOGETHER FOR GOOD TO THOSE WHO LOVE GOD, TO THOSE WHO ARE THE CALLED ACCORDING TO HIS PURPOSE."

Romans 8:28

o you feel entirely free to pursue the plan and purpose you believe God has for your life? Do you think that if something is truly "right" it should be error-free and happen quickly and effortlessly? Are you hindered by a feeling that there's just one "right way" to do something?

The woman who has true freedom to pursue her purpose is a woman who is free to laugh at her own foibles and mistakes, even as she seeks to do her best. She is a woman who is free from the pressure to be perfect.

Patsy Clairmont reminds us that we live in a world filled with mistakes, which can be the basis for some of our greatest memories:

> Have you ever attended a wedding where a mishap didn't occur? In the midst of lace, netting, white roses,

and lit candles someone passes out, throws up, says the wrong name, sings off key, or forgets their cue. . . .

Or what about having company over for dinner? The house is sparkling from all your efforts, the table setting looks like it's right out of *House Beautiful*, and the aroma of food is scrumptious. In fact, it's so heavenly when you go to check on the rolls, you find Fido on a chair wolfing down your glorious pineapple-studded ham. As you scream, he quickly takes one more mouthful and scampers for cover, flinging bits of your dinner in his path. . . .

I have to remind myself that we live in a fallen world and that nothing is going to be perfect here. Everything is slightly askew.

— Patsy Clairmont

1. Can you recall an incident in your life that seemed like a disaster at the time, but which has made for a great memory or an opportunity for lots of laughter since then?

2. In what ways do you tend to take yourself too seriously or expect too much of yourself?

3. Read the words of Jesus in Matthew 6:25–31 below. Circle the words or phrases that seem to stand out to you as you read this passage:

> [Jesus said,] "Therefore I say to you, do not worry about your life, what you will eat or what you will drink; nor about your body, what you will put on. Is not life more than food and the body more than clothing? Look at the birds of the air, for they neither sow nor reap nor gather into barns; yet your heavenly Father feeds them. Are you not of more value than they? Which of you by worrying can add one cubit to his stature? So why do you worry about clothing? Consider the lilies of the field, how they grow: they neither toil nor spin; and yet I say to you that even Solomon in all his glory was not arrayed like one of these. Now if God so clothes the grass of the field, which today is, and tomorrow is thrown into the oven, will He not much more clothe you, O you of little faith? Therefore do not worry, saying, 'What shall we eat?' or 'What shall we drink?' or 'What shall we wear?'"

4. Is it easy or difficult for you to be unconcerned with details associated with your appearance? What if you are attempting to impress someone you admire, someone you consider to be influential, or someone who is in authority over you?

When a person comes to God, just as she is—while still in her sinning state—God looks at her and, because of what Jesus Christ did on the Cross, He proclaims her righteous. She does not have to clean up her act. She does not have to do penance. She does not have to be thin or good-looking or rich or famous or accomplished. All she has to do is believe God for the forgiveness of her sins.

Luci Swindoll

5. What do you do when you feel "embarrassed" about a mistake you have made?

So what's the difference? Why do I sometimes get bogged down with chores, hating the day? Then, at other times, I get fired up with enthusiasm, loving the day? Perspective! Perspective is everything.

Luci Swindoll

How do you *wish* you could handle mistakes or embarrassment?

6. Eve was the only woman who ever lived in a perfect world—and even Eve saw that world collapse as the result of her own bad choices (see Genesis 3:16–19). Describe how you believe Eve must have felt after she had been expelled from the Garden of Eden and found herself living in a world in which the ground was cursed and filled with thorns and thistles, her husband had to toil to put bread on their table, and she was under the "rule" of her husband as never before?

How do you believe Eve must have felt as she experienced pain for the first time, saw herself aging, and had to be concerned about the care of clothing—all for the first time?

7. In what ways do you struggle when your best efforts do not produce the perfection you desire?

As most of us read through Jesus's Sermon on the Mount, we get "stuck" on what Jesus said in Matthew 5:48—"You shall be perfect, just as your Father in heaven is perfect." Perfect? How can we let go of worry that is related to perfectionism if Jesus said we are to be *perfect*? However, this statement in the Greek language, in which the New Testament was written, may have been translated: "Reflect the nature of God to the extent that you are humanly capable of doing so, and treat others as God would treat them."

8. Two other translations of this verse are below. What insights do these different translations give you?

Live generously and graciously toward others, the way God lives toward you. (MSG)

You, therefore, must be perfect [growing into complete maturity of godliness in mind and character, having reached the proper height of virtue and integrity], as your heavenly Father is perfect. (AMP)

*J*esus gave balance to what it means to be "perfect" when He said, "Why do you call Me good? No one is good but One, that is, God" (Matthew 19:17). Jesus expected people to obey God's commandments and to reflect God's character, but He also knew that human beings make mistakes, even those who seek to be godly at all times. Not only does God recognize that we aren't perfect, but He's already paid the price for our shortcomings and He loves us in spite of them.

9. What can happen to a person who expects perfection in herself?

What can happen to a person who expects perfection from other people?

> *Never resist His insistence on your perfection. He is working all things together for good, not just for you and yours, but for people you've never met and may not meet until your paths cross in heaven.*
>
> Barbara Johnson

+DIGGING DEEPER+

As you pursue your life's dream and purpose, have you built in some "space and time" for correcting mistakes, dealing with technical difficulties, or handling unavoidable interruptions? Take some time to revisit your goals and the timetables you have set for reaching them. Consider ways you might build in some "down time" or "recovery time" to accommodate life's unavoidable crises.

✦ PONDER AND PRAY ✦

In what ways do you feel challenged in your spirit to talk to God about your perfectionist tendencies? Are you really willing to trust God to turn all things for your good?

✦ NOTES & PRAYER REQUESTS ✦

CHAPTER 5

FREEDOM FROM INSECURITY

"I WILL PRAISE YOU, FOR I AM FEARFULLY AND WONDERFULLY MADE."

Psalm 139:14

o you know what your talents are—the unique combination of abilities that God has built into you from birth? Have you caught a glimpse of your unlimited potential and all the ways in which you might still grow, develop, and accomplish good things for God's glory? If you haven't yet discovered your God-given talents and abilities, now is the time!

The Bible tells us that every person is given natural abilities, that every Christian is given spiritual gifts, and that God has an eternal plan and purpose for the use of all the gifts He imparts to us. In other words, God made you exactly as you are, for a very special role on this earth. It's no accident that you have *your* personality, *your* abilities and capabilities, *your* skills, and a unique just-for-you set of circumstances in which to be fully who you are . . . to the max! This sets us free from being chained to a life of insecurity, wishing we had the talents and gifts of others.

And there's more good news! It is never too late to explore your potential, your gifts, and the ways in which you might use them. Patsy Clairmont has drawn great encouragement from some women who are doing amazing things after their one-hundredth birthday! They are not concerned with who society says they should be or what they should do—instead, they walk in the paths God made for them. Let their examples encourage you:

> How about one-hundred-year-old Mahilda, who signed her name on the ticket to be a California gubernatorial candidate? She said she didn't like the way they were doing things. You go, girl.
>
> While Mahilda is politicking, centenarian Inez from Minnesota had her first solo art show. Inez, you're proof it's never too late to brushstroke one's dreams into reality.
>
> Lonnie, also a sprightly one hundred years old, continues, after years in the educational system as a teacher and principal, to make important contributions. Now she's part of a Philanthropic Education Association, which owns a college and fosters the education of women. What a legacy . . .
>
> We never get so old that we can't try something we've never done before to keep ourselves current, fresh, and connected to those around us.
>
> —Patsy Clairmont

1. If you don't know what your unique talents and gifts are, how might you discover them? Here's an exercise to help you dig deeper. Think back to when you were a little girl . . .

What did you most want to do on a Saturday or during vacations from school?

What did you never tire of playing?

What did you most enjoy studying in school?

> *God tells us that He knew us in our mother's womb. He tells us that He knows us, even better than we know ourselves. And best of all, He knows something beyond what we know: He knows what He is calling us to become.*
>
> Nicole Johnson

What were you really good at doing?

What did you look forward to doing anytime you could?

2. Are you doing today what gave you pleasure and success as a child or teenager? If not, why not? What might you do to fold those activities into your life once again?

3. Psalm 139:13–18 is a tremendous Bible passage about the way in which each person is "fearfully and wonderfully made." As you read this passage, how does it make you feel that God has fashioned you uniquely, and with the utmost care?

4. God knows more about your talents and abilities than you likely know! He knows you better than you know yourself.

Read Psalm 139:1–6.

What abilities do you *suspect* God may have placed in you—that perhaps you have been reluctant or unable to discern so far?

What might you do to begin to explore those potential talents or gifts?

*S*he may appear to be a "perfect woman"—but on close examination, the woman described in Proverbs 31 represents a list of individual traits with which most women can relate in *some way* . . . (though not likely in *all* ways). This woman apparently enjoyed shopping, gourmet cooking, gardening, physical fitness activities, beautiful clothes, and volunteer work. How do *you* relate to her?

5. As you read through the passage below, write notes to yourself about ways in which you believe this woman to be the "impossible dream"—or ways in which you believe she is a very practical representation of your life.

> Who can find a virtuous wife?
> For her worth is far above rubies.
> The heart of her husband safely
>   trusts her:
> So he will have no lack of gain.
> She does him good and not evil
> All the days of her life.
> She seeks wool and flax,
> And willingly works with her hands.
> She is like the merchant ships,
> She brings her food from afar.
> She also rises while it is yet night,
> And provides food for her household,
> And a portion for her maidservants.
> She considers a field and buys it;
> From her profits she plants a vineyard.
> She girds herself with strength,
> And strengthens her arms.

The Creator has made us each one of a kind. There is nobody else exactly like us, and there never will be. Each of us is His special creation and is alive for a distinctive purpose. Because of this, the person we are, and the contribution we make by being that very person, are vitally important to God.

Luci Swindoll

She perceives that her merchandise is good,
And her lamp does not go out by night.
She stretches out her hands to the distaff,
And her hand holds the spindle.
She extends her hand to the poor,
Yes, she reaches out her hands to the needy.
She is not afraid of snow for her household,
For all her household is clothed with scarlet.
She makes tapestry for herself;
Her clothing is fine linen and purple.
Her husband is known in the gates,
When he sits among the elders of the land.
She makes linen garments and sells them,
And supplies sashes for the merchants.
Strength and honor are her clothing;
She shall rejoice in time to come.
She opens her mouth with wisdom,
And on her tongue is the law of kindness.
She watches over the ways of her household,
And does not eat the bread of idleness.
Her children rise up and call her blessed;
Her husband also, and he praises her.

(Proverbs 31:10–28)

6. Identify five traits that you believe to be at the core of *your* virtuous nature.

✦DIGGING DEEPER✦

Identify several of your traits—personality traits, talents, skills—that qualify you in a distinctive way for pursuing your goals and dreams.

✦PONDER AND PRAY✦

If you find yourself reluctant to identify or embrace the unique gifts God has built into you as a woman, talk to God about why. If you are reluctant to develop a certain gift, ask God to help you identify your fears and to help you overcome them. If you have misjudged a gift or talent . . . ask God to correct your understanding of yourself and to direct you toward those things that are truly your giftedness.

✦ NOTES & PRAYER REQUESTS ✦

CHAPTER 6

FREEDOM TO EXPLORE YOUR UNIQUE PURPOSE

"SHOW ME THE WAY I SHOULD GO, FOR TO YOU
I LIFT UP MY SOUL."

Psalm 143:8 NIV

Every woman has a unique purpose on the earth, a unique role to fill, a unique set of tasks to accomplish. There's amazing freedom in knowing who you are, and then in doing what you know to do!

The true reason you are on this earth may be different from what you once thought your purpose would be. The role you always thought you might fulfill may not be at all what God has actually asked you to do.

This doesn't mean that God doesn't still have certain roles, relationships, and opportunities ahead for you. It does mean that right where you are, and as you are, God has a very specific purpose for you to fulfill. Real freedom comes when a woman chooses to find her unique niche in whatever circumstance she finds herself.

Barbara Johnson has written about one young woman who didn't get what she necessarily wanted . . . but she got much more:

> At her small, rural high school, cheerleaders for the basketball team were elected by a vote of the student population. She'd been on the squad the previous two years, so it was especially hard when her junior year began and she wasn't reelected. The election took place in the morning, and she had a hard time enduring the rest of that long, sad school day, her young heart broken as she felt her fellow students' rejection and thought of all the fun she would be missing the next year as her friends carried on with their enthusiastic cheerleading. . . .
>
> The next day at lunchtime, the basketball coach asked her if she would be the team's statistician during the coming season. She quickly agreed.
>
> Her new position meant she still got to ride the bus with the cheerleaders and basketball players to all the games, and, she said, "I got lots more attention from the boys on the team when I was statistician than I ever had as cheerleader, because the players always wanted to know their stats. I had to keep track of every shot attempted—where it was made from and whether the shot was good—and I had to figure percentages for each player, how many field goals or free throws were attempted, and how many were made. So suddenly all the boys on the team were always wanting to talk to me!"
>
> The experience was a life lesson for that young woman. It taught her to look for something good in the difficult experiences that have come her way since then, knowing that God's plan is to prosper her and to give her hope. It reminded her that even when setbacks and challenges occur, she must be patient and wait for the next step of the plan to unfold.

Decide to accept the path God has given you with courage, grace, and humor. Don't deny reality, but choose to think on what is excellent and praiseworthy.

Luci Swindoll

In a strange but marvelous way, her belief gives her a sense of freedom because she knows she doesn't have to figure out the big picture by herself. She doesn't have to see how each piece of her life fits into God's big, glorious picture. She just keeps believing. Keeps praying. Keeps trusting. And she knows that in the end, God's plan will be revealed to her, and she'll be able to see her life as God sees it.

—Barbara Johnson

1. Have you ever been disappointed that something didn't turn out the way you'd hoped—but then something even better happened?

2. In what ways do you struggle when you don't see how all the pieces of your life fit into "God's big, glorious picture"?

In what ways do you struggle to "keep believing" and to "keep trusting"?

3. What do these verses of Scripture tell you about your ability to see your life as God sees you?

1 Corinthians 13:12

1 Corinthians 4:4–5

Psalm 31:19

4. What do these verses tell you about the surety of God's plan and purpose coming to fruition in your life?

Habakkuk 2:3

1 Thessalonians 5:23–24

Psalm 31:14–16

5. God's Word gives us abundant encouragement to wait for God's best timing and methods. The very essence of a walk of faith is to believe that God will reveal His purposes to us as we "step out." He gives us light for one step at a time.

What do the verses below tell us about God's faithfulness?

Hebrews 11:3

Lamentations 3:25

Galatians 6:9–10

> *Live every day to fulfill your personal mission. God has a reason for whatever season you are living through right now. A season of loss or blessing? A season of activity or hibernation? A season of growth or incubation? You may think you're on a detour, but God knows the best way for you to reach your destination.*
>
> Barbara Johnson

*M*ary, the mother of Jesus, is a woman who no doubt envisioned a different life for herself than the one she eventually led. As a young girl in Israel, she would never have imagined that she might become pregnant by the power of the Holy Spirit after she was betrothed to Joseph. She would never have imagined a journey to Egypt and back. She would never have imagined that her baby boy would one day die by Roman crucifixion.

6. Has your "role" in life turned out the way you envisioned it when you were a young teenager? What is different? What is the same?

How have you coped with the differences?

*J*esus knew His purpose. The prophet Isaiah foretold it centuries before His birth:

"The Spirit of the Lord GOD is upon Me, because the LORD has anointed Me to preach good tidings to the poor; He has sent Me to heal the brokenhearted, To proclaim liberty to the captives, And the opening of the prison to those who are bound; to proclaim the acceptable year of the LORD, And the day of vengeance of our God; to comfort all who mourn, to console those who mourn in Zion, To give them beauty for ashes, The oil of joy for mourning, The garment of praise for the spirit of heaviness; That they may be called trees of righteousness, The planting of the LORD, that He may be glorified." (Isaiah 61:1–3)

7. As a follower of Christ, what does it mean to you personally to have the purpose that Jesus had?

Apply Isaiah's phrases below to your own life. What can they mean for you?

Preach good tidings to the poor:

Heal the brokenhearted:

Proclaim liberty to the captives:

Open the prison to those who are bound:

Proclaim the acceptable year of the LORD:

Comfort and console those who mourn:

Put on the garment of praise for the spirit of heaviness:

Be called a tree of righteousness and a planting of the LORD:

✦Digging Deeper✦

Look back to what you wrote about your life's dream in the first lesson. Then look at the traits and gifts you've identified in Chapter 5. Can you put your life's purpose into a short statement—perhaps thirty words or less?

✦Ponder and Pray✦

In what ways do you need God's help as you identify your life's purpose? Ask Him for that help!

> *God sees you just as you are, he loves you just the way you are, and he has a purpose for you.*
>
> Sheila Walsh

✦ Notes & Prayer Requests ✦

CHAPTER 7

FREEDOM TO MAKE YOUR OWN CHOICES

"CHOOSE FOR YOURSELVES THIS DAY WHOM YOU WILL SERVE."

Joshua 24:15a

Many of the choices we face are not a matter of good and bad—most women know to choose good and turn away from bad. The choices are more often choices between good and best. Many of the choices we face are not a matter of what is right for all one's life, but what is right for this one season of life.

The woman who is free is a woman who chooses what is best, not only in her eyes, but in the eyes of the Lord. She has a freedom born of confidence that she is doing what will help her fulfill her God-given dreams and purpose.

To what degree do you feel that you have freedom to choose between the workplace and home? To what degree do you feel free to choose the tasks that occupy your day? To what degree do you feel free to take on some responsibilities and delegate others?

Thelma Wells says:

> Many people are looking for absolute freedom. Freedom from fear, anxiety, sickness, hopelessness, poverty, ignorance, negative emotions, insecurity, disharmony, joblessness—you name it, we want freedom from it. But we cannot experience complete and total freedom without some constraints. To be free to do whatever we want is to become a slave to lack of discipline, laziness, and sin.
>
> Our purpose in life is not to shun our responsibilities as model citizens or to become lazy about any other obligations, but to be free to live out our God-given assignments.
>
> —Thelma Wells

1. What are some of the choices you are facing today that are related to your specific "God-given assignments"?

Can you foresee a day in which your God-given assignment might take on a new facet or move in a new direction? What "new choices" might you face at that time?

$\mathcal{T}$he Bible has a great deal to say about the choices we make. Choices are at the heart of setting priorities, scheduling days, and deciding the ways in which we are going to discipline our bodies, minds, and emotions. One of the most famous Bible passages about choice-making is below. Moses was calling upon the Israelites to make choices that involved very specific consequences — choices not unlike ones we face today.

2. What insights do you have into the passage below?

> I call heaven and earth as witnesses today against you, that I have set before you life and death, blessing and cursing; there-fore choose life, that both you and your descendants may live; that you may love the LORD your God, that you may obey His voice, and that you may cling to Him, for He is your life and the length of your days; and that you may dwell in the land which the LORD swore to your fathers, to Abraham, Isaac, and Jacob, to give them. (Deuteronomy 30:19–20)

Dear friend, embrace your day—this day—it is a gift. Take the LORD's [small cap] hand. He will help you unwrap the day and then celebrate it. And His grace will be sufficient for any need you have.

Patsy Clairmont

Consider these phrases in particular:

• "Choose life." Some decisions involve physical life and death. Some of the choices we make involve emotional life or death, or the "life or death" of a relationship, job, ministry, or position. What does it mean to you to choose life?

• "That you may love the LORD . . . obey His voice . . . and cling to Him." In what ways are your choices related to your ability to freely and fully love, trust, and obey God?

3. What do these Bible passages tell us about our decision-making?

Joshua 24:15

Proverbs 1:28–31

Mark 8:18

*T*he Old Testament prophet Ezekiel was given a word from God about how not to make choices for one's life: "For the king of Babylon stands at the parting of the road, at the fork of the two roads, to use divination: he shakes the arrows, he consults the images, he looks at the liver" (Ezekiel 21:21). All of these are examples of "divination"—of looking at specific signs in the natural world and making a decision based upon man's opinions about the way things "look."

4. In what ways do you base your decisions on assumptions or on opinions about the way things "appear" to be?

What should you base your decisions upon instead?

*E*ve was a woman who made a terrible choice. She disobeyed God in choosing to eat the fruit from a tree that God had said was "off limits" to her and to Adam (see Genesis 2:16–17; 3:1–6). Take a closer look at what enticed Eve to eat from this tree.

5. How prone are we to the temptations Eve faced?

Satan promised Eve, "you will be like God." In what ways would you like to be more "like God"? (For example, to have God's power to heal or to have God's ability to know what lies in the future.) In what ways does your desire to be more like God make you vulnerable to certain temptations?

How can a person find strength to say "no" to things that the world says are good, even when God says they aren't?

$\mathcal{G}$od told Adam and Eve that the consequence for eating from the tree of the knowledge of good and evil was this: "in that day that you eat of it you shall surely die" (Genesis 2:17). God wanted Adam and Eve to know only good . . . not evil. He wanted them to experience only those things that were related to life . . . not death. Although Adam and Eve did not physically die on the day they ate of the forbidden fruit, they began to age immediately toward an inevitable conclusion of death.

6. What "dies" in a person when she willfully chooses what God has forbidden?

In what ways does Jesus's promise of everlasting life in John 3:16 give hope that all good things in us might come to life as we believe in Him?

*T*he Bible says of itself that all Scripture is given for our benefit. What God commands us to do is for both our earthly and eternal good.

7. Note your insights into the passage below, which calls us to use Scripture as our basis for making choices and decisions that result in good:

> Every Scripture is God-breathed (given by His inspiration) and profitable for instruction, for reproof and conviction of sin, for correction of error and discipline in obedience, [and] for training in righteousness (in holy living, in conformity to God's will in thought, purpose, and action), So that the man of God may be complete and proficient, well fitted and thoroughly equipped for every good work. (2 Timothy 3:16–17 AMP)

8. What do the verses below mean to you as you seek to make godly choices and decisions?

Matthew 7:7

James 1:5–6

✦Digging Deeper✦

As you journey toward your God-given dreams and purpose, you will face countless choices and decisions. To better prepare yourself for those times, write out the steps you should take when faced with a "fork in the road." (For example, "I will go to God's Word first to find out if God has anything to say about this decision" or, "I will pray until I have peace about my choice—I won't act until I know that I'm doing what God says is right for me.")

✦Ponder and Pray✦

What choice or decision do you need to talk to God about today?

✦ Notes & Prayer Requests ✦

_____

_____

_____

_____

_____

_____

_____

_____

CHAPTER 8

FREEDOM TO SET BOUNDARIES

"[JESUS SAID,] 'WHAT GOOD WOULD IT DO TO
GET EVERYTHING YOU WANT AND LOSE YOU,
THE REAL YOU? WHAT COULD YOU EVER
TRADE YOUR SOUL FOR?'"

Mark 8:36–37 MSG

Most of us know the physical boundaries of our personal space or the boundaries of our home. At work, we know the boundaries of our office space, our sales "territory," and the boundaries associated with the tasks we have been assigned. In society, we know the laws that govern our behavior. But when it comes to emotional boundaries, we are sometimes adrift. We agree to things we don't really want, we buy things we don't really need, and at times we say "yes" to commitments when we really need to say "no."

Have you set good boundaries in your relationships with other people? Have you set boundaries regarding your use of time and talent? Have you set boundaries about what you will take into your heart and mind?

Barbara Johnson writes about recognizing boundaries associated with things that are both "important" and "unimportant":

One thing about cancer: it frees you from all the unimportant stuff in your life. Suddenly, that two-page to-do list that's been burdening you all week is replaced by a couple of simple, over-riding priorities: keep breathing, and keep believing.

I've always been one who looks for the joy in whatever predicament I find myself in, so when I got the cancer diagnosis, I was determined to find something joyful in it. And sure enough, I discovered that I now have a great excuse for not doing all the things I didn't really want to do but for which I somehow ended up on the list of volunteers. Once you've been through a couple of rounds of chemo or a few doses of radiation, no one expects you to bring a casserole to the church's potluck or a plate of cookies to Bible study. You're completely excused from hosting the garden club and can instead be a gracious guest and compassionately indulged moocher at just about any function you care to attend . . .

In the process, it brings us freedom to focus entirely on what is most important.

— Barbara Johnson

1. Is there something in your life today that you wish you had said "no" to?

What keeps you from saying "no" now?

How much courage does it take to say "no" to a request from some-one you admire? From someone who has authority over you, such as a supervisor at work or the chairman of a committee on which you serve?

$\mathcal{M}$any of the boundaries that the Bible calls us to set involve relationships and associations—especially rela-tionships among believers, and those between an unbe-liever and a believer in Christ. Two of the most famous passages are found below.

2. The apostle Paul was not an isolationist, but he did teach that we are to set limits on the degree to which we allow those with different beliefs to influence us:

> Do not be unequally yoked together with unbelievers. For what fellowship has righteousness with lawlessness? And what communion has light with darkness? And what accord has Christ with Belial [a name for the devil]? Or what part has a believer with an unbeliever? And what agreement has the temple of God with idols? For you are the temple of the living God. As God has said:

"I will dwell in them
And walk among them.
I will be their God,
And they shall be My people."
Therefore
"Come out from among them
And be separate, says the Lord.
Do not touch what is unclean,
And I will receive you."
"I will be a Father to you,
And you shall be My sons and daughters,
Says the LORD Almighty."

(2 Corinthians 6:13–18)

Is there anyone in your life who consistently encourages you to doubt God or yourself? How do you think this verse applies to that relationship?

Don't let anyone rob you of your confidence in God. Know His Word. Hold on to His hand. He will make your impossible mission possible and your life so much more bearable.

Barbara Johnson

3. The apostle Paul also gave clear directive about how we are to work together with other people in the body of Christ:

> For as we have many members in one body, but all the members do not have the same function, so we, being many, are one body in Christ, and individually members of one another. Having then gifts differing according to the grace that is given to us, let us use them . . .
>
> Let love be without hypocrisy. Abhor what is evil. Cling to what is good. Be kindly affectionate to one another with brotherly love, in honor giving preference to one another; not lagging in diligence, fervent in spirit, serving the Lord; rejoicing in hope, patient in tribulation, continuing steadfastly in prayer; distributing to the needs of the saints, given to hospitality.
>
> Bless those who persecute you; bless and do not curse. Rejoice with those who rejoice, and weep with those who weep. Be of the same mind toward one another. Do not set your mind on high things, but associate with the humble. Do not be wise in your own opinion.
>
> Repay no one evil for evil. Have regard for good things in the sight of all men. If it is possible, as much as depends on you, live peaceably with all men.
>
> (Romans 12:3–6a; 9–18)

What do you believe the balance to be between considering the input and welfare of another person and maintaining your own emotional boundaries and sense of personal identity?

4. Two women in the New Testament church at Philippi had very different opinions and were at odds with each other. The apostle Paul wrote to them, "I implore Euodia and I implore Syntyche to be of the same mind in the Lord. And I urge you also, true companion, help these women who labored with me in the gospel" (Philippians 4:2–3a).

> Have you ever struggled in your relationship with another Christian woman? Was it a matter of a boundary being violated? Were you, or the other woman, making decisions that weren't yours to make, taking on responsibilities that didn't belong to you, or requiring things that weren't required by God? What ultimately happened in this relationship?

> What boundaries might God be calling you to "reset" in this or other relationships?

5. Every day, we are bombarded by countless messages that are not in line with God's commandments or His desire to bless us. Many of these messages call upon us to "be tolerant," even of things we know are evil. Deciding what you believe—really believe at the core of your being—can set you free from doubt. Knowing what you believe with unwavering assurance can free you from countless frustrations and debates.

*L*uci Swindoll had an experience in setting and maintaining boundaries about what she truly believes. She writes:

> This morning I was looking at a small oil painting that hangs in my breakfast room and began to contemplate the friend who painted it . . . we were neighbors about forty years ago. . . .
>
> I always enjoyed her company. We talked about literature, art, music, travel, families, books, gardening . . . all the things that held a fascination for us both. . . . Sadly, the most important thing in my life meant absolutely nothing to her.
>
> One evening we talked about how life is full of sorrows and heartache and queried how any of us can go through . . . loss without totally giving up. I mentioned there was no way to explain it except that God made it possible. [She] looked at me and made the most interesting comment: "You know, Luci, one day down the road . . . let's say ten years . . . you won't believe in God either. When you're older and wiser in the ways of the world, God will mean nothing more to you than a figment of your imagination. If you want to be free of anything, you have to set yourself free. He doesn't exist, and the sooner you realize that, the stronger person you'll be inside. That's the way it works."
>
> . . . A lot about me has changed since the mid-1960s. My views have altered on issues about life. I've learned more about the world. I've grown more tolerant of people and their circumstances. I've realized I don't have to prove everything I believe. But other things are just like they were back then. I'm still collecting art, still plowing my way through the Durants' *Story of Civilization*, still enjoying a winter's evening with friends . . . but most of all, I still believe in God. More than ever.
>
> You know how I know that? Because I have peace about God in my heart. His Spirit rings true with my spirit, and he has kept his word over and over. There is a validation inside that can't be had if belief is not present. I've learned the truth

about God, and that truth has set me free — free to be me, free
to love him, free to live fully by his grace.

I can't really explain this freedom he's provided . . . not to
me and certainly not to [my friend]. I just know I feel it deeply
and love the fact of that feeling. My relationship with God
has been tested and deepened and lengthened and enhanced
through living, suffering, aging, losing, and loving . . . all that
and more. He's very much there, strong in my heart, mind,
and spirit. We're hanging out together all the time, he and I. I
know all that about me for sure.

— Luci Swindoll

6. It is often in the midst of a challenge to our beliefs that we discover
our boundaries. Has anyone ever challenged you to give up what you
believe about Jesus? Where did you draw the line, defining what you
know to be true?

7. Identify three or four core beliefs you have about God and your
relationship with Him — beliefs that have remained unshaken through
difficult circumstances over the years.

8. How are you sure of your beliefs? What confirms your beliefs to you? How have those clear boundaries helped you deal with doubt?

9. How do you know when you should consider changing what you have always believed in the past?

How can you tell when changes in the "boundaries" of a relationship or a belief are changes the Lord may be prompting you to make?

10. As you read the passages of Scripture below, note what these verses reveal to you about areas in which a person must "stand fast":

Philippians 1:27

Philippians 4:1

2 Thessalonians 2:15

✦DIGGING DEEPER✦

Walking the good road toward the fulfillment of your God-given dreams and purpose means, in part, staying on the road! All good roads have clear, bordered edges. Staying on the road also means not taking unproductive or ungodly detours. Identify several potential "detours" that you need to avoid taking. (Note: they might include the "path of procrastination" or the "lane of lust" or the "street of selfish desires.")

✦ PONDER AND PRAY ✦

Consider the big-issue questions for which you don't seem to have a definitive answer. Ask the Lord to reveal His answer to you.

✦ NOTES & PRAYER REQUESTS ✦

✦ Notes & Prayer Requests ✦

CHAPTER 9

FREEDOM TO BE SPONTANEOUS AND MAKE MID-COURSE CORRECTIONS

"THE RACE IS NOT TO THE SWIFT, NOR THE BATTLE
TO THE STRONG, NOR BREAD TO THE WISE, NOR RICHES
TO MEN OF UNDERSTANDING, NOR FAVOR TO MEN OF
SKILL; BUT TIME AND CHANCE HAPPEN TO THEM ALL."

Ecclesiastes 9:11

Have you ever found yourself face to face with what you know needs to be a "mid-course correction"? Do you ever grow weary of the grind, racing toward your goals, wishing and fantasizing about a day off just to play? Do you find yourself feeling uptight when your schedule is interrupted . . . even if you know the interruption couldn't be avoided? Do you find yourself tensing up at the word *surprise*? Do you wish you could be more spontaneous but just don't know how?

The word *rigid* stands at the opposite end of the spectrum from freedom! Just as perfectionism tends to keep a woman from feeling free as she pursues her God-given dreams and purpose, so does having an inflexible attitude. Not all circumstances can be controlled, not all situations can be managed fully! The truly free woman trusts God to be in charge of her day—her plans and her schedule—and to use even delays, interruptions, and detours to her benefit. The woman who is free allows for spontaneity and has an ability to "go with the flow" of life around her, even as she stands firm in character and keeps her eyes fixed on her goals.

Nicole Johnson has described an incident that would delight some women and perhaps cause panic in others. How would you respond?

I heard their laughter in the hallway first. The door opened, and three young, professional women walked through the door of the day spa where I was getting a quick manicure. . . . They were all carrying briefcases and were apparently there for some sort of business appointment. Bonnie asked to speak to someone, and then Bonnie and her friends stood around chatting and waiting for the person they had requested. But when a woman came out with a white terrycloth robe and slippers for Bonnie and took her briefcase and handbag in exchange, Bonnie's two friends started laughing and clapping.

Needless to say, I was terribly curious. I can smell a celebration, even through nail polish remover, and I was dying to know what was going on. They were there for another fifteen minutes or so, and then the two friends departed and Bonnie was taken into the spa. After the commotion subsided, I asked the receptionist what had happened. She said that the friends had booked their

There are occasions when my perfectly laid plans don't work for me. Why? Interruptions! Unexpected delays. Circumstances out of my control. That's when I have to make a choice—either lose my mind (and my decorum!), or look beyond my puny plan and see if God has something different or even better in store.

Luci Swindoll

coworker, Bonnie, for a day at the spa as a surprise. They had set up a "day of meetings" and were coming to their first "appointment" to meet with the director of the spa, who happened to be a real client of the firm that all three women worked for. When the woman came out to see them carrying a robe and slippers, it was then that Bonnie's friends informed her they had cleared her calendar, and the "day of meetings" had been replaced by scheduled spa treatments, including a facial and massage.

—Nicole Johnson

1. Do you like surprises? Why . . . or why not?

Many women don't like surprises, but the truth is, life is filled with surprises—some wonderful and some not-so-wonderful. Mary, the mother of Jesus, was no doubt surprised when her husband Joseph told her that he had been warned in a dream by an angel who said, "Arise, take the young Child and His mother, flee to Egypt, and stay there until I bring you word; for Herod will seek the young Child to destroy Him." The Bible tells us that the family left "by night" (see Matthew 2:13–14).

2. How would you have responded if you had been Mary, who by this time in her life had already relocated from Nazareth to Bethlehem and was likely still a teenager with a toddler son? Would you have responded quickly without questions or reluctantly with many questions?

3. How open are you to the idea of "mid-course corrections"?

I realized how tart I become when inconvenienced. It doesn't take much of a breeze to topple me. I want to believe that, if called upon to be a heroine, I would rise to the occasion. But experience has proven me feeble.

Patsy Clairmont

When you have made your plans carefully, how irritated do you get with delays or interruptions?

*M*any people believe that "planning" and "spontaneity" are opposites. They aren't. Planning can actually
allow a person to be more spontaneous in the moment.
In fact, a day "off" from diligently working toward a goal
may be just the right medicine for infusing new energy
and creativity into a plan. A person who has a plan always
has a reference point to which she can return.

4. Read James 4:13–15. Can you recall an incident in your life in which
something did *not* go as you planned, and you later discovered that the
Lord seemed to engineer the changes for your benefit, just as He did for
Mary and Joseph?

5. When it comes to the fulfillment of your dreams and purpose, in
what ways do you feel challenged by Romans 8:28 — "We know that all
things work together for good to those who love God, to those who are
the called according to His purpose"?

*T*he apostle Paul writes:

Not that I have already attained, or am already perfected; but I press on, that I may lay hold of that for which Christ Jesus has also laid hold of me. . . . I do not count myself to have apprehended; but one thing I do, forgetting those things which are behind and reaching forward to those things which are ahead, I press toward the goal for the prize of the upward call of God in Christ Jesus. (Philippians 3:12–14)

6. How does "discipline" differ from "rigidity"?

To what extent do all plans need to be flexible?

7. The Bible has several key passages that relate directly to the way we pursue our dreams and purposes. Note your insights into each of the passages below:

1 Corinthians 9:24–27

Hebrew 12:1–3

Matthew 7:24–26

Matthew 25:1–12

✦Digging Deeper✦

Do you have a plan for turning your dreams and purpose into reality? How might you better prepare yourself emotionally for dealing with delays, unexpected obstacles, or detours as you pursue your dreams and goals?

Write down two or three sentences of "commitments to myself" for handling potential crises. In writing these statements before a crisis occurs, you are likely to be better prepared for handling a crisis when it arises.

✦Ponder and Pray✦

In what ways do you feel challenged to ask God to help you "roll with the punches," never losing sight of your goals and dreams but at the same time, refusing to get uptight when every day doesn't turn out as you planned it?

✦ Notes & Prayer Requests ✦

CHAPTER 10

FREEDOM FROM THE SHACKLES OF WORRY

"I HAVE LEARNED THE SECRET OF BEING CONTENT IN ANY AND EVERY SITUATION."

Philippians 4:12 NIV

Garden-variety fears tend to show up in our lives as worry or anxiety. A woman who walks in true freedom may feel "butterflies" from time to time—and she certainly may have concerns—but she refuses to allow anxiety or worry to hold her back. Are you anxious or worried today? Do you know why? Every woman seems to have a different reason for anxiety. Thelma Wells writes about an experience in her life:

> Instead of following through on all my well-intentioned plans, I found myself with a sickness that confined me to bed. . . .
>
> My sickness did not worry me one bit. No, it was lying in bed that got on my last nerve. It was depending on other people for everything I needed. It was the humiliating experience of not being able to do things for myself that I'd done for other people all my life. My worry was that I was not any service to anybody, not even to myself.
>
> —Thelma Wells

1. What do you worry about?

> *When somebody calls me with bad news, or my kids call me with problems they're facing, I ask myself, "What does the Word say?" Don't worry about it. Be anxious for nothing. Why shouldn't we worry about it? Because worry says to God, "Lord, I don't trust You." But we do worry, and then what?*
>
> Thelma Wells

Do you worry "routinely" or just on rare occasions?

2. Is there anything that is "worth" worry? Is there a way to live without worry? The apostle Paul wrote about anxiety. Note your insights into his words below:

> Be anxious for nothing, but in everything by prayer
> and supplication, with thanksgiving, let your requests
> be made known to God; and the peace of God, which
> surpasses all understanding, will guard your hearts and
> minds through Christ Jesus. (Philippians 4:6–8)

Note especially these two phrases:

• "Be anxious for nothing."

How difficult is this? What is necessary for a person to be anxious for *nothing*?

• "By prayer and supplication, with thanksgiving." How important is the role of giving thanks in overcoming worry?

Identify a specific worry in your life.

Now list three things related to that worry for which you are *very thankful*:

Spend a few minutes thanking God for His goodness in the past and praising Him for His power over all people and situations. What impact does offering thanks and praise have on your feelings of anxiety?

3. Paul went on to tell the Philippians of positive things they should think about instead of "worry thoughts." Again, note your insights. Then give an example for each of the praiseworthy categories in this passage.

> Whatever things are true, whatever things are noble,
> whatever things are just, whatever things are pure,
> whatever things are lovely, whatever things are of
> good report, If there is any virtue and if there is
> anything praiseworthy—meditate on these things.
> The things which you have learned and received and
> heard and saw in me, these do, and the God of peace
> will be with you. (Philippians 4:8–9)

Consider these phrases in particular:

• "Meditate on these things." To meditate means to ponder repeatedly. In a very practical, concrete way, what does it mean to you to "meditate"?

• "The things you have learned . . . received . . . heard . . . saw in me, these do. Who are your role models for a successful Christian life, one free of anxiety and worry? What do your role models teach, give, tell, or model that is worthy of your imitation?

$\mathscr{P}$aul wrote in a similar vein to the Romans, saying, "So here's what I want you to do, God helping you: Take your everyday, ordinary life—your sleeping, eating, going-to-work, and walking-around life—and place it before God as an offering. Embracing what God does for you is the best thing you can do for him" (Romans 12:1–2 MSG).

4. What does it mean to you to give your daily life to the Lord as an "offering?"

5. What insights do these Bible passages give us about anxieties and "cares"?

1 Peter 5:6–7

Mark 4:14,18–19

Matthew 6:31–33

Matthew 6:34

erhaps the epitome of "anxiety" in the New Testament is a woman named Martha. Jesus came to her home on one occasion, and the Bible says that she was "distracted with much serving," and all the while, her sister, Mary, sat at the feet of Jesus, listening intently to His every word. Frustrated by what she perceived to be Mary's lack of help, Martha said to Jesus, "Do You not care that my sister has left me to serve alone? Therefore tell her to help me." Jesus replied, "Martha, Martha, you are worried and troubled about many things. But one thing is needed, and Mary has chosen that good part, which will not be taken away from her" (see Luke 10:38–42). It wasn't that Jesus didn't appreciate Martha's serving or that He didn't think there was an appropriate time for serving. Rather, Jesus appreciated Mary's priority on worshipful listening and learning.

Sometimes, despite our best intentions, we find ourselves wandering in a wilderness of anxiety, lost and unable to find our way out. I know. For years I felt that way. Nothing seemed to work; I felt stripped and anxious, unable to determine what my mission in life should be.

Thelma Wells

6. In what ways does anxiety over a situation keep you from hearing what Jesus might desire to say to you?

How important is it to listen *first*—as a top priority—to what Jesus says, before we act? In what ways is it important to listen to Jesus as a means of "preventing" undue worry about whether we are doing the right thing?

✦DIGGING DEEPER✦

In what ways does the pursuit of your purpose inevitably involve facing anxiety and learning to deal with it?

✦PONDER AND PRAY✦

In what areas of your life do you feel challenged to ask God to help you cast all of your "cares" upon Him?

✦ Notes & Prayer Requests ✦

✦ Notes & Prayer Requests ✦

CHAPTER 11

FREEDOM TO SPEAK UP

"MEN AND BRETHREN, LET ME SPEAK FREELY TO YOU . . ."

Acts 2:29

very woman desires to be heard and to have her words heeded. Tremendous freedom comes to the woman who gives voice to her ideas, feelings, and beliefs . . . and to the woman who believes she is worthy to be heard. Tremendous satisfaction comes to the woman whose opinion is followed with good results.

How much freedom do you have to express your ideas, opinions, and feelings? How effective are you in your communication? A key part of "speaking up" is simply being heard. Marilyn Meberg knows:

> The first year Ken and I were married, I was teaching the third grade and Ken was in graduate school. My meager salary paid the rent as well as his tuition. I felt that alone would earn a listening ear from time to time. One evening as we sat eating our tuna casserole, I made the casual comment that the dog with rabies was back on the playground again. Ken didn't seem to hear

me, so I said, "The principal was bitten as he tried to chase the dog off. It was a horrible sight, especially since the principal started foaming at the mouth this morning during our faculty meeting." Silence.

I put my head over Ken's plate and stared into his face, only a few inches from mine, and I could see him trying to swallow a laugh. "Marilyn, has it come to this . . . you have to make up a story about a rabid dog and a principal foaming at the mouth to get my attention?"

Soberly I said, "I've been reduced to wild storytelling, and it's your fault. Who knows what I may say to someone who is actually listening to me?"

—Marilyn Meberg

1. If you aren't being "heard" today, what are some of the potential reasons?

A key part of "speaking up" doesn't really involve speaking at all. It means first listening or learning so that when you speak, you speak with accuracy and conviction and empathy. The Bible gives important insights into listening and learning as vital aspects of communication.

2. What insights do these Bible passages give us about communication?

Proverbs 13:1–3

Proverbs 15:1–2, 4

Proverbs 16:23

*Q*ueen Esther in the Bible was bold in speaking up—and her words saved her people, the Jews, from death. Before Esther spoke, however, she listened to her relative, Mordecai. When Esther heard distressing stories about Haman's behavior, she sent a trusted messenger to Mordecai asking "what and why" (see Esther 4).

3. How did Mrdecai respond to Esther's request for information?

Identify a situation about which you would like to know "what and why"?

From whom might you get the information you desire?

$\mathcal{H}$ow and when a woman speaks is as critical as what a woman says. Proverbs 15:23b says, "A word spoken in due season, how good it is!"

Esther certainly knew this to be true. She responded to Mordecai's "what and why" information by telling him that she could not see the king any time she wanted—she needed to be summoned into the king's presence and he hadn't sent for her in thirty days. Mordecai responded with urgency, advising her that she must not remain silent or she would perish along with all other Jews. Esther again sent word to Mordecai, asking him to have all the Jews in Shushan fast and pray for her, and telling him that she and her maids would do the same (see Esther 4:10–17).

4. Identify a situation in which timing and methodology were critically important in conveying information. What happened?

What factors go into discerning the "right" time to speak up and the "right" methods to use?

5. What might be gained by having prayer support from other people as you prepare to speak up?

Proverbs 25:11 says, "A word fitly spoken is like apples of gold in settings of silver." This verse has great depths of meaning:

Apple: likely a pomegranate, a fruit rich in taste, texture, and beauty; the seeds of a pomegranate are a symbol of collective wisdom and truth.

Gold: an extremely valuable substance; in Bible times, small amounts of pure gold were often molded into various shapes.

Setting: context

Silver: a valuable substance often used as a means of exchange in business transactions

This verse could be translated: "A well-chosen word is like a beautiful and fruitful expression of truth, molded for maximum effectiveness in the context of an important conversation."

6. When might it be important to craft what you say very carefully in order to have maximum effectiveness?

Are you facing a situation today in which every word is important? Why?

Queen Esther's first message to her husband, the king, was a nonverbal one. She put on her royal robes and stood in the inner court of the king's palace to catch the king's eye (see Esther 5:1). When he summoned her, she invited him to a banquet in her private chambers.

7. In what ways are nonverbal messages important when you "speak up" about important matters?

In what ways was Esther's banquet a nonverbal form of communication? What messages did the banquet likely convey?

What are some of the reasons it might be important to arrange a private time to speak up?

The way in which we communicate often speaks louder than what we say. Words spoken in anger, bitterness, hatred, or resentment sting . . . often, with lasting, ongoing pain.

8. Those who speak in loud, angry, or cynical ways often are heard . . . but not with the best results. How do you feel when someone speaks to you in a loud, angry, or cynical voice?

At the second feast that Queen Esther provided for her husband, the king, and his wicked advisor, Haman, the king invited Esther to make a petition. She began her request by saying, "If I have found favor in your sight, O king, and if it pleases the king, let my life be given me at my petition, and my people at my request" (Esther 7:3). Esther went on to tell the king that if the issue involved only slavery, she would not have brought it up, but since the issue involved life and death, she felt she had to speak. The king asked who would dare kill Esther and her people. She boldly named her enemy (see Esther 7:4–6).

9. What tone of voice do you believe Esther used as she made her request?

In communicating, why is it important to state precisely the outcome you desire and to speak in a way that demonstrates respect for another person's authority?

In communicating, why is it important to have pure motives? Attempts at manipulation always seem to become obvious the longer a person with impure motives speaks. Can you recall an example of this in your experience?

✦Digging Deeper✦

James is a book in the New Testament that has a great deal to say about the ways in which we are to communicate as Christians. Read James 3:2–12. This passage is something like a "Code of Conduct for Godly Communication." Having a good "Code of Conduct" for communication can be very beneficial to you in the pursuit of your dreams and purpose. Good communication can make your path easier, your journey faster, and your achievements greater. List several messages that you consider to be absolutely necessary for you to communicate now or in the near future. Next to each item you list, write down how you believe you should communicate that message.

✦Ponder and Pray✦

Prayer is "talking things over" with God. What are you feeling the need to "talk over" with God when it comes to the way you speak to others, when you voice your ideas and opinions, and what you believe to be important to say?

✦ Notes & Prayer Requests ✦

CHAPTER 12

FREEDOM TO LOVE AND BE LOVED

"[JESUS SAID,] 'THESE THINGS I HAVE SPOKEN TO YOU,
THAT MY JOY MAY REMAIN IN YOU, AND THAT YOUR JOY
MAY BE FULL. THIS IS MY COMMANDMENT, THAT YOU
LOVE ONE ANOTHER AS I HAVE LOVED YOU.'"

John 15:11–12

*G*reat freedom is experienced by the woman who easily expresses feelings of genuine and godly love! Every woman knows how "free" she feels—enthusiastic and joyful—when she knows that someone loves her.

The good news is that we don't have to be told we are loved in order to feel love. We can tell others we love them and show them we love them by doing things to honor and value them. In the speaking and showing of love we feel love in our own hearts! How much love do you have in your life? Is it possible you need to be voicing your love in new ways and more often? Nicole Johnson writes:

> When we are deeply loved, we have the greatest freedom known to man. Love gives us wings and lets us take flight. It is this freedom that a life journey with

Christ produces in us. It's not that after years of walking with God we feel we are "better"; hopefully, we are freer. We are set free to pour out love and grace and mercy on others out of the abundant supply of love that is given freely to us.

> *Beloved, let us love one another, for love is of God; and everyone who loves is born of God and knows God. He who does not love does not know God, for God is love.*
>
> 1 John 4:7–8 NKJV

And we can see the contrast. People who do not know love in the core of their being are stingy in their hearts. They seek to hoard the little love they have for fear it will be taken away from them. In actuality, the reverse is true. Love shrinks in response to hoarding and fear, which in turn multiplies the mistrust and anxiety.

But to allow the love of God to take hold of us and to possess our hearts with its strength and beauty is to unlock the prison of fear and usher us into the freedom of being able to love others. We are no longer poor; we are no longer paupers with nothing to offer. We have been given the riches of heaven, and we are free to live like kings, lavishing love and care on all those around us.

—Nicole Johnson

1. To what extent have you allowed the love of God to "take hold" of you and give you freedom in your ability to express love to others?

2. Over time, in what ways have you grown in your ability to show love to other people? In what ways has expressing love become more difficult?

The Bible has a great deal to say about God's love for us. God's love is given to us first, and it becomes the basis on which we not only love Him, but love others. As John wrote, "We love Him because He first loved us," (1 John 4:19) and "he who loves God must love his brother also" (1 John 4:21).

3. What insights do these passages of Scripture give us about the love God has for each of us?

1 John 4:16

1 John 4:12

1 John 3:16–18

Romans 8:35

The Bible tells of two extraordinary women who poured out their love in different ways to Jesus. One of them is an unnamed woman described as a "sinner" who knew that Jesus was at the home of a certain religious leader in the city. Before the feast in this man's home began, she went to Jesus and knelt before Him, weeping. She literally washed His feet with her tears and wiped them with the hair of her head. She then kissed His feet and anointed them with a fragrant oil she had brought in a flask. Jesus recognized that this woman's display of love was a genuine act of repentance and of faith. He said to her, "Your sins are forgiven. . . . Your faith has saved you. Go in peace" (see Luke 7:36–50). The religious leader who was hosting the dinner criticized Jesus for allowing this woman to lavish such attention on Him. The reply Jesus made follows on the next page.

> *Let's enter into the love adventure of our lives and seek creative ways of telling our awesome God, "We love You! We thank You! We will live for You!"*
>
> Sheila Walsh

4. What does the verse below tell us about the way God desires for us to express our love?

> [Jesus said,] "I entered your house; you gave Me no water for My feet, but she has washed My feet with her tears and wiped them with the hair of her head. You gave Me no kiss, but this woman has not ceased to kiss My feet since the time I came in. You did not anoint My head with oil, but this woman has anointed My feet with fragrant oil. Therefore I say to you, her sins, which are many, are forgiven, for she loved much. But to whom little is forgiven, the same loves little." (Luke 7:44–47)

*T*he second woman noted in the Bible for her act of love toward Jesus was Mary, the sister of Lazarus and Martha. A short while after Jesus raised Lazarus from the dead, he was having supper with Martha, Mary, and Lazarus. Mary took a pound of very costly oil of spikenard, poured it over the feet of Jesus, and then wiped His feet with her hair. One of the disciples criticized her for doing this, saying she should have taken the oil and sold it and given the money for the care of the poor (it would have been worth about a year's wages). Jesus refused to criticize her, but rather, honored her act as one of love (see John 12:1–8).

5. What are some practical ways for a woman to show love to Jesus today?

*L*uci Swindoll writes about a practical way she likes to express joy and love to others:

I love to cook, am crazy about new recipes, and am known to try add-ons when it comes to whipping up a soufflé, meatloaf, or casserole. It's all about the freedom to have fun and enjoy good fellowship. . . .

Sometimes the most ordinary activities become opportunities to have fun when we feel free to express ourselves. We enjoy the process, connect with friends, and give ourselves the freedom to create memories that will ensure a feeling of joy and nostalgia many years down the road. Don't worry about getting everything right as much as having a good time. Consider camaraderie and conversation . . . conviviality and celebration . . . all the while creating memories with those you love!

—Luci Swindoll

5. What are some practical ways you can show love to one another?

7. Is it easier for you to "show" love or to say, "I love you?" Why?

Now is the time to live as Christ lived. Now is the time to love as Christ loved.

Sheila Walsh

✦Digging Deeper✦

No journey of faith toward the fulfillment of one's God-given dreams and purpose is worth much if it isn't a journey marked with overflowing love—both love received and love expressed. Make a list of people to whom you feel a need to say "I love you." Then next to each person's name, put a practical way you might express your love to that person, or write a short statement of what you might say to the person to express your love. Then, take action! Express your love. Do you feel a new degree of freedom after expressing love? It just may be that the dreams and purpose you desire most for your life are fulfilled as you express your love in words and deeds.

✦Ponder and Pray✦

Express your love to the Lord today. Tell Him how much He means to you. Ask Him to help you show your love to others in a way that sets both you and them free.

✦ Notes & Prayer Requests ✦

✦Leader's Guide✦

A Note to Leaders

As the leader of a small discussion group, think of yourself as a facilitator—someone who can "get the discussion started" and who seeks to involve every person in the group. You certainly don't need to be the person with all the answers! In truth, many of the questions asked in this study do not have precise answers. Your role is to encourage an open, candid discussion that remains focused on the Bible.

At the beginning of your study, emphasize to the group that your goal as a group is to gain new insights into God's Word—the goal is not to be a forum for defending a point of doctrine or a theological opinion. Stay focused on what God's Word says and what it means. The purpose of a group study is also to share insights with each other on how to apply God's Word to everyday life. *Every* person in the group can and should contribute—the collective wisdom that flows from Bible-focused discussion is often very rich and deep.

Seek to create an environment in which every member of the group feels free to ask questions of other members in order to gain greater understanding. Encourage the group members to voice their appreciation to one another for new insights gained, and to be supportive of one another personally.

You may want to start a study session by asking the group, "What really impacted you most in this lesson?" Additional questions to start your discussion might be:

- Was there a particular part of the lesson, or a question, that you found troubling?

- Was there a particular part of the lesson that you found encouraging or insightful?

- Was there a particular part of the lesson that you'd like to explore further?

Since many of the questions in this study do not require an "answer" but are more reflective and personal in nature, answers are not listed in this Leader's Guide. However, Bible verses are associated with a number of the questions in this guide. If the full text of the passage is not included in the lesson itself, you'll find it below.

Also as part of the material below, you'll find additional questions not asked in the lessons. You may want to reserve some time in your group meeting for discussing one or more of these additional questions if they apply to your group discussion. Have a great study!

Chapter 1: Freedom to Dream

2. John 16:23b–24 — "Whatever you ask the Father in My name He will give you. Until now you have asked nothing in My name. Ask, and you will receive, that your joy may be full."

3. Ephesians 3:20a says that God "is able to do exceedingly abundantly above all that we ask or think."

4. Matthew 21:22, "Whatever things you ask in prayer, believing, you will receive." John 15:7–8, "If you abide in Me, and My words abide in you, you will ask what you desire, and it shall be done for you. By this My Father is glorified, that you bear much fruit; so you will be My disciples." James 4:3, "You ask and do not receive, because you ask amiss, that you may spend it on your pleasures."

7. Isaiah 1:18–19, "Come now, and let us reason together," says the LORD, "Though your sins are like scarlet, they shall be as white as snow; though they are red like crimson, they shall be as wool. If you are willing and obedient, you shall eat the good of the land." Psalm 86:5, "For You, Lord, are good, and ready to forgive, and abundant in mercy to all those who call upon You." John 10:10, "The thief does not come except to steal, and to kill, and to destroy. I have come that they may have life, and that they may have it more abundantly."

9. First Corinthians 2:9–10, "'Eye has not seen, nor ear heard, nor have entered into the heart of man the things which God has prepared for those who love Him.' But God has revealed them to us through His Spirit. For the Spirit searches all things, yes, the deep things of God." Proverbs 3:5–6, "Trust in the LORD with all your heart, and lean not on your own understanding; in all your ways acknowledge Him, and He shall direct your paths." Jeremiah 42:2b–3, "Please, let our petition be acceptable to you . . . that the LORD your God may show us the way in which we should walk and the thing we should do." Habakkuk 2:2, "Write the vision and make it plain on tablets, that he may run who reads it."

Additional questions for reflection or discussion:

• What do you think is the difference between a fantasy and a dream?

• Why do you think a lot of people are afraid to dream "big dreams"?

• Why do you think that more of our dreams don't become reality?

Chapter 2: Freedom from Paralyzing Fears

1. Second Timothy 1:7—Consider specifically what it means to you to have power, love, and a sound mind. Psalm 31:13–14—Consider various ways we sometimes allow other people to assume the role of "God" in our lives—at least from the perspective that they have power over us or that we fear their control. What can a person do to regain the right perspective about who is truly "in charge" of all things? Hebrews 13:5b–6—Consider the ways a woman gains courage from truly believing that Jesus never rejects nor forsakes her? Consider the ways a woman might feel freer after she confronts "the worst that another person can do to me"?

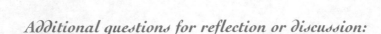

Additional questions for reflection or discussion:

- Have you ever truly learned anything or become a "pro" at anything without some moments of failure or fear along the way?

- How do you know when you are experiencing God's peace?

Chapter 3: Freedom from Sorrow and Painful Memories

9. Revelation 21:4, "And God will wipe away every tear from their eyes; there shall be no more death, nor sorrow, nor crying. There shall be no more pain, for the former things have passed away. Then He who sat on the throne said, 'Behold, I make all things new.'"

Additional questions for reflection and discussion:

- How do you respond to others when you feel sorrowful? Are you open and eager to share with someone, or do you tend to retreat from others?

- What do you think are some of the reasons people are often reluctant to reach out to someone who seems to be sorrowful?

- Do you know somebody today whom you suspect needs your comfort in a time of sorrow? What do you believe God wants you to do for them?

Chapter 4: Freedom from Perfectionism

Additional questions for reflection or discussion:

- To what extent is a "perfect" world always impacted in a negative way by pain, flawed relationships with other people, and material concerns?

- The flip side of perfectionism is often the "blame game"—blaming others for a lack of perfection. How can a person guard against playing the blame game?

- Do you struggle with perfection as you grow older and begin to see imperfections, wrinkles, and graying hair?

Chapter 5: Freedom from Insecurity

3. Psalm 139:13–18, "For You formed my inward parts; You covered me in my mother's womb. I will praise You, for I am fearfully and wonderfully made; Marvelous are Your works, And that my soul knows very well. My frame was not hidden from You, When I was made in secret. And skillfully wrought in the lowest parts of the earth. Your eyes saw my substance, being yet unformed. And in Your book they all were written, The days fashioned for me, When as yet there were none of them. How precious also are Your thoughts to me, O God! How great is the sum of them! If I should count them, they would be more in number than the sand; When I awake, I am still with You.

4. Psalm 139:1–6, "O LORD, You have searched me and known me. You know my sitting down and my rising up; You understand my thought afar off. You comprehend my path and my lying down, And are acquainted with all my ways, For there is not a word on my tongue, But behold, O LORD, You know it altogether. You have hedged me behind and before, And laid Your hand upon me. Such knowledge is too wonderful for me; It is high, I cannot attain it."

Additional questions for reflection or discussion:

• Is there a dream that you once had for your life that you now feel is too late to pursue? Why? Is there a way that dream might be adapted or altered now so that you can go for it?

Chapter 6: Freedom to Explore Your Unique Purpose

3. First Corinthians 13:12, "Now we see in a mirror, dimly, but then face to face. Now I know in part, but then I shall know just as I also am known." First Corinthians 4:4–5, "For I know of nothing against myself, yet I am not justified by this; but He who judges me is the Lord. Therefore judge nothing before the time, until the Lord comes, who will both bring to light the hidden things of darkness and reveal the counsels of the hearts. Then each one's praise will come from God." Psalm 31:19, "Oh, how great is Your goodness, which You have laid up for those who fear You, which You have prepared for those who trust in You in the presence of the sons of men!"

4. Habakkuk 2:3, "For the vision is yet for an appointed time; but at the end it will speak, and it will not lie. Though it tarries, wait for it; because it will surely come, it will not tarry." First Thessalonians 5:23–24, "Now may the God of peace Himself sanctify you completely; and may your whole spirit, soul, and body be preserved blameless at the coming of our Lord Jesus Christ. He who calls you is faithful, who also will do it." Psalm 31:14–16, "But as for me, I trust in You, O LORD; I say, 'You are my God.' My times are in Your hand; deliver me from the hand of my enemies, and from those who persecute me. Make Your face shine upon Your servant; save me for Your mercies' sake."

5. Hebrews 11:3, "By faith we understand that the worlds were framed by the word of God, so that the things which are seen were not made of things which are visible." Lamentations 3:25, "The LORD is good to those who wait for Him, to the soul who seeks Him." Galatians 6:9–10, "Let us not grow weary while doing good, for in due season we shall reap if we do not lose heart. Therefore, as we have opportunity, let us do good to all, especially to those who are of the household of faith."

Additional questions for reflection or discussion:

• How does a "dream" differ from a "purpose"? (Hint: one deals with "what," the other with "why.")

• Is it possible to lead a genuinely purpose-filled life without Christ Jesus?

Chapter 7: Freedom to Make Your Own Choices

3. Joshua 24:15, "And if it seems evil to you to serve the LORD, choose for your-selves this day whom you will serve, whether the gods which your fathers served that were on the other side of the River, or the gods of the Amorites, in whose land you dwell. But as for me and my house, we will serve the LORD." Proverbs 1:28–31, "Then they will call on me, but I will not answer; they will seek me diligently, but they will not find me. Because they hated knowledge and did not choose the fear of the LORD, they would have none of my counsel and despised my every rebuke. Therefore they shall eat the fruit of their own way, and be filled to the full with their own fancies." Mark 8:18, "[Jesus said,] 'Having eyes, do you not see? And having ears, do you not hear? And do you not remember?'"

6. John 3:16, "For God so loved the world that He gave His only begotten Son, that whoever believes in Him should not perish but have everlasting life."

8. Matthew 7:7, "[Jesus said,] 'Ask, and it will be given to you; seek, and you will find; knock, and it will be opened to you. For everyone who asks receives, and he who seeks finds, and to him who knocks it will be opened.'" James 1:5–6, "If any of you lacks wisdom, let him ask of God, who gives to all liberally and without reproach, and it will be given to him. But let him ask in faith, with no doubting, for he who doubts is like a wave of the sea driven and tossed by the wind."

Additional questions for reflection and discussion:

• In what ways do God's acts of provision and protection for you in the past provide a foundation for your decision-making?

• In what ways is it important for you to truly to understand the whole of God's Word in order to make wise choices?

Chapter 8: Freedom to Set Boundaries

9. Philippians 1:27, "Only let your conduct be worthy of the gospel of Christ, so that whether I come and see you or am absent, I may hear of your affairs, that you stand fast in one spirit, with one mind striving together for the faith of the gospel." Philippians 4:1, "Therefore, my beloved and longed-for brethren, my joy and crown, so stand fast in the Lord, beloved." Second Thessalonians 2:15, "Therefore, brethren, stand fast and hold the traditions which you were taught, whether by word or our epistle."

Additional questions for reflection and discussion:

• How important is it that two believers have the "same mind in the Lord?" Does this mean that all believers should have the same "doctrine" or "style?" On what matters should believers have the same mind in the Lord?

• How can a person go about setting "new boundaries" for a relationship that has had "old boundaries" for years . . . perhaps decades?

• Where do you "draw the line" about what you will change in your behavior? Your long-standing habits? Your thinking or opinions? Your believing or faith?

Chapter 9: Freedom to Be Spontaneous and Make Mid-Course Corrections

5. James 4:13–15 — Come now, you who say, "Today or tomorrow we will go to such and such a city, spend a year there, buy and sell, and make a profit"; whereas you do not know what will happen tomorrow. For what is your life? It is even a vapor that appears for a little time and then vanishes away. Instead you ought to say, "If the Lord wills, we shall live and do this or that."

8. 1 Corinthians 9:24–27, "Do you not know that those who run in a race all run, but one receives the prize? Run in such a way that you may obtain it. And everyone who competes for the prize is temperate in all tings. Now they do it to obtain a perishable crown, but we for an imperishable crown. Therefore I run thus: not with uncertainty. Thus I fight: not as one who beats the air. But I discipline my body and bring it into subjection, lest, when I have preached to others, I myself should become disqualified." Hebrew 12:1–3, "Therefore we also, since we are surrounded by so great a cloud of witnesses, let us lay aside every weight, and the sin which so easily ensnares us, and let us run with endurance the race that is set before us, looking unto Jesus, the author and finisher of our faith, who for the joy that was set before Him endured the cross, despising the shame, and has sat down on the right hand of the throne of God. For consider Him who endured such hostility from sinners against Himself, lest you become weary and discouraged in your souls." Matthew 7:24–26, "[Jesus said,] 'Therefore whoever hears these sayings of Mine, and does them, I will liken him to a wise man who built his house on the rock: and the rain descended, the floods came, and the winds blew and beat on that house; and it did not fall, for it was founded on the rock. But everyone who hears these sayings of Mine, and does not do them, will be like a foolish man who built his house on the sand: and the rain descended, the floods came, and the winds blew and beat on that house; and it fell. And great was its fall.'" Matthew 25:1–12, "[Jesus said,] 'Then the kingdom of heaven shall be likened to ten virgins who took their lamps and went out to meet the bridegroom. Now five of them were wise, and five were foolish. Those who were foolish took their lamps and took no oil with them, but the wise took oil in their vessels with their lamps. But while the bridegroom was delayed, they all slumbered and slept. And at midnight a cry was heard: "Behold, the bridegroom is coming; go out to meet him!" Then all those virgins arose and trimmed their lamps. And the foolish said to the wise, "Give us some of your oil, for our lamps are going out." But the wise answered, saying, "No, lest there should not be enough for us and you; but go rather to those who sell, and buy for yourselves." And while they went to buy, the bridegroom came, and those who were ready went in with him to the wedding; and the door was shut. Afterward the other virgins came also, saying, "Lord, Lord, open to us!" But he answered and said, "Assuredly, I say to you, I do not know you."' "

Additional questions for reflection or discussion:

• Respond to this statement: The best spontaneity is the spontaneity within the borders of a plan.

• Think of a time when you needed to "stand firm" and not bend. Then think of a time when you needed to bend rather than "stand firm." How did you know which to do?

Chapter 10: Freedom from the Shackles of Worry

5. First Peter 5:6–7, "Therefore humble yourselves under the mighty hand of God, that He may exalt you in due time, casting all your care upon Him, for He cares for you." Mark 4:14,18–19, "The sower sows the word. . . . Now these are the ones sown among thorns; they are the ones who hear the word, and the cares of this world, the deceitfulness of riches, and the desires for other things entering in choke the word, and it becomes unfruitful." Matthew 6:31–33, "[Jesus said,] 'Therefore do not worry, saying, "What shall we eat?" or "What shall we drink?" or "What shall we wear?" For after all these things the Gentiles seek. For your heavenly Father knows that you need all these things. But seek first the kingdom of God and His righteousness, and all these things shall be added to you.'" Matthew 6:34, "[Jesus said,] 'Therefore do not worry about tomorrow, for tomorrow will worry about its own things. Sufficient for the day is its own trouble.'"

Additional questions for reflection and discussion:

• Respond to the statement: Worry is a form of fear.

• Do you think that constant worrying reflects a lack of trust in God?

• How does being a chronic worrier impact your Christian witness?

Chapter 11: Freedom to Speak Up

2. Proverbs 13:1–3, "A wise son heeds his father's instruction, but a scoffer does not listen to rebuke. A man shall eat well by the fruit of his mouth, but the soul of the unfaithful feeds on violence. He who guards his mouth preserves his life, but he who opens wide his lips shall have destruction." Proverbs 15:1–2, 4, "A soft answer turns away wrath, but a harsh word stirs up anger. The tongue of the wise uses knowledge rightly, but the mouth of fools pours forth foolishness. . . . A wholesome tongue is a tree of life, but perverseness in it breaks the spirit." Proverbs 16:23, "The heart of the wise teaches his mouth, and adds learning to his lips.

Additional questions for reflection and discussion:

• Respond to the old saying: "Sticks and stones may break my bones but words will never hurt me."

• Can you ever really "take back" words that you have spoken in anger or bitterness?

• If an issue involves a third party, as in Esther's case, what are some of the reasons you might benefit from having a meeting that includes the "problem person"? When might you benefit from not having such a person present?

• What do you believe to be the balance between speaking with urgency and conviction, and speaking in a way that allows the other person the privilege of making the final decision?

Chapter 12: Freedom to Love and Be Loved

3. First John 4:16, "We have known and believed the love that God has for us. God is love, and he who abides in love abides in God, and God in him." First John 4:12b, "If we love one another, God abides in us, and His love has been perfected in us." First John 3:16–18, "By this we know love, because He laid down His life for us. And we also ought to lay down our lives for the brethren. But whoever has this world's goods, and sees his brother in need, and shuts up his heart from him, how does the love of God abide in him? My little children, let us not love in word or in tongue, but in deed and in truth." Romans 8:35, "Who shall separate us from the love of Christ? Shall tribulation, or distress, or persecution, or famine, or nakedness, or peril, or sword?"

Additional questions for reflection or discussion:

• What is the most loving thing a friend has ever said to you?

• What is the most loving thing a friend has ever done for you?

✦ NOTES ✦

✦ Notes ✦

THE COMPLETE WOMEN OF FAITH®
STUDY GUIDE SERIES

WOMEN OF FAITH *Amazing*

FREEDOM

2007

"So if the Son makes you free, you will be truly free." — John 8:36

We often catch *GLIMPSES OF FREEDOM* but what about the *promise* of being truly free? That's *AMAZING!* Women of Faith...as always, *FRESH, FABULOUS,* and *FUN-LOVING!*

*2007 Conference Schedule**

March 15 - 17
San Antonio, TX

April 13 - 14
Little Rock, AR

April 20 - 21
Des Moines, IA

April 27 - 28
Columbus, OH

May 18 - 19
Billings, MT

June 1 - 2
Rochester, NY

June 8 - 9
Ft. Lauderdale, FL

June 15 - 16
St. Louis, MO

June 22 - 23
Cleveland, OH

June 29 - 30
Seattle, WA

July 13 - 14
Washington, DC

July 20 - 21
Chicago, IL

July 27 - 28
Boston, MA

August 3 - 4
Ft. Wayne, IN

August 10 - 11
Atlanta, GA

August 17 - 18
Calgary, AB Canada

August 24 - 25
Dallas, TX

September 7 - 8
Anaheim, CA

September 14 - 15
Philadelphia, PA

September 21 - 22
Denver, CO

September 28 - 29
Houston, TX

October 5 - 6
San Jose, CA

October 12 - 13
Portland, OR

October 19 - 20
St. Paul, MN

October 26 - 27
Charlotte, NC

November 2 - 3
Oklahoma City, OK

November 9 - 10
Tampa, FL

November 16 - 17
Phoenix, AZ**

**There will be no Pre-Conference in Phoenix.

FOR MORE INFORMATION CALL **888-49-FAITH**
OR VISIT **WOMENOFFAITH.COM**
*Dates, Time, Location and special guests are subject to change.
Women of Faith is a ministry division of Thomas Nelson Publishers.*